MW00358537

For the Teacher

This reproducible study guide consists of lessons to use in conjunction with a specific novel. Written in chapter-by-chapter format, the guide contains a synopsis, pre-reading activities, vocabulary and comprehension exercises, as well as extension activities to be used as follow-up to the novel.

In a homogeneous classroom, whole class instruction with one title is appropriate. In a heterogeneous classroom, reading groups should be formed: each group works on a different novel on its reading level. Depending upon the length of time devoted to reading in the classroom, each novel, with its guide and accompanying lessons, may be completed in three to six weeks.

Begin using NOVEL-TIES for guided reading by distributing the novel and a folder to each child. Distribute duplicated pages of the study guide for students to place in their folders. After examining the cover and glancing through the book, students can participate in several pre-reading activities. Vocabulary questions should be considered prior to reading a chapter or group of chapters; all other work should be done after the chapter has been read. Comprehension questions can be answered orally or in writing. The classroom teacher should determine the amount of work to be assigned, always keeping in mind that readers must be nurtured and that the ultimate goal is encouraging students' love of reading.

The benefits of using NOVEL-TIES are numerous. Students read good literature in the original, rather than in abridged or edited form. The good reading habits will be transferred to the books students read independently. Passive readers become active, avid readers.

Novel-Ties® are printed on recycled paper.

SYNOPSIS

As a resident of the cozy Mountain View Inn, Ralph S. Mouse leads a happy, sheltered life. He is the proud owner of a shiny red motorcycle, a gift from a young hotel guest. His favorite pastime is speeding down the hallways at night, feeling the wind in his whiskers. Matt, the inn's kindly handyman, looks out for Ralph and keeps him well supplied with snacks.

Ralph's idyllic life is interrupted one winter when a rowdy crew of outdoor mice invades the inn. These interlopers, as well as Ralph's indoor siblings and cousins, crowd around him each night, demanding rides on his beloved motorcycle. Besides bothering Ralph, the pesky mice leave footprints and droppings in the lobby, causing the manager to threaten Matt with dismissal.

Desperate to save Matt's job and enjoy his motorcycle in peace, Ralph convinces his friend Ryan, the housekeeper's son, to take him along as a stowaway on the school bus. That is how the adventurous rodent takes up residence in Room 5 of Irwin J. Sneed Elementary School.

Though Ralph tries to remain hidden in his friend's pocket, Ryan's classmates soon discover the small furry visitor. Room 5's enthusiastic teacher, Miss Kuchenbacker—Miss K for short—is so enchanted with Ralph that she decides to make him the center of a class project on mice. Ralph, however, is reluctant to be part of Ryan's contribution to the mouse exhibit, a maze that he is to build with his classmate Brad Kirby. To induce the mouse to be more cooperative, Ryan confiscates Ralph's motorcycle.

After quarreling with Brad, Ryan constructs the maze at home by himself. This disappoints Ralph, who had hoped to practice running the maze at night so he could perform well on the big day.

On the day of the "Great Mouse Exhibit," Ralph's fear of humiliation becomes a self-fulfilling prophecy. Because there are so many competing odors in the classroom, Ralph cannot smell the peanut butter that is supposed to lead him to the exit in the maze. Frustrated, the mouse climbs to the top of the partition and runs along the top edges of the walls until he reaches the peanut butter. Brad taunts Ryan for having a "dumb" pet, and in the ensuing scuffle, Ryan falls down, breaking Ralph's precious motorcycle, which is in his pocket.

After Ralph spends a mournful weekend alone at school, the class returns on Monday. During a discussion, the students come to a consensus that Ralph's solution to

the maze is, in fact, evidence that he is a "gifted and talented" mouse. The class reads with disbelief in the *Cucaracha Voice*, a local newspaper, that their school is infested with mice and that the school superintendent has promised to investigate the "mouse plague." The students are incensed about these inaccuracies in an article that was written by a reporter who had made a superficial visit to the mouse exhibit. Ralph fears that he may become the victim of a full-scale mouse hunt. Fortunately, the school does not have funding for more than a few mousetraps, which are no threat to a smart mouse like Ralph. The students write indignant letters to the newspaper editor, who then retracts the mouse infestation story.

After confronting one another over the broken toy motorcycle, Ryan and Brad reveal the problems in their own lives, thus forging a new friendship, partially based on the loneliness each experiences. As reparation for the broken motorcycle, Brad gives Ralph a sleek, mouse-sized sports car.

Ryan brings Brad to the inn to play, and when Brad's father comes to pick him up in his tow truck, he meets Ryan's mom. The two parents fall in love and marry, making Ryan and Brad stepbrothers as well as friends.

PRE-READING QUESTIONS AND ACTIVITIES

1. Preview this book by reading the title and the author's name and by looking at the illustration on the cover. What do you think the book will be about? Do you think it will be funny or serious? Will it be a fantasy or a realistic story? Have you read any other books by the same author? Have you read any other books about Ralph S. Mouse? If so, discuss the story lines of each of these books with your classmates.

2. The book *Ralph S. Mouse* is a sequel to Beverly Cleary's book *The Mouse and the Motorcycle*. Brainstorm with your classmates who have read this book to find out about Ralph, his human friend Ryan, and the Mountain View Inn where they live.

3. Part of *Ralph S Mouse* takes place at an inn, a kind of hotel. Before you read the book, find out what each hotel worker, listed in the chart below, does at work. Use a dictionary or ask an adult for information.

Job Title	Job Description
desk clerk	
housekeeper	
bellboy	
manager	
maid	
handyman	

4. **Science Connection:** Do some research about mice. Find out about the habits and lifecycle of fieldmice and house mice.

5. Create a classroom display of toy vehicles, such as cars, trucks, and motorcycles. Determine which ones a mouse could drive. If possible, place toy mice in the vehicles. This will help you understand the activities of Ralph S. Mouse as you read the book.

6. Assemble a "We Like Mice" bulletin board. Include drawings, photocopies of book illustrations, magazine and Internet photos, fables, folk and fairy tales, nursery rhymes, song lyrics, and poems about mice.

7. Conduct a class survey to find out what kinds of pets your classmates own. Which kind of pet is most popular? Which pet is most unusual? Does anyone have a pet mouse?

   With a partner, list your favorite mouse characters in books and movies. Write a one-sentence description of each. As you read *Ralph S. Mouse*, think about ways that Ralph's personality and adventures are similar to those of other fictional mice.

8. As you read *Ralph S. Mouse*, fill in the following story map.

Story Map
Title
Author
Main character
Other characters
Settings

Ralph's problems	Solutions to Ralph's problems

How the story ends

CHAPTER 1

Vocabulary: Draw a line from each word on the left to its definition on the right. Then use the numbered words to fill in the blanks in the sentences below.

1. rodents

2. keen

3. retired

4. defiant

5. venture

6. reproach

7. winced

8. civilized

    a. went to bed

    b. dare to go

    c. showing a refusal to obey

    d. animals such as rats, mice, or squirrels

    e. very sharp or sensitive (in seeing, hearing, smelling, or tasting)

    f. polite; taught to have good manners

    g. pulled or moved away from something painful or dangerous

    h. blame

. . . .

1. Like other _____, beavers have strong front teeth that they use for gnawing.

2. When I accidentally touched the hot frying pan, I _____ in pain.

3. Rabbits will not _____ out of their burrows until they are sure it is safe.

4. We were so tired Friday night that we _____ early.

5. Warthogs cannot see very well, but they have _____ senses of smell and hearing.

6. My grandma says that _____ people do not eat with their elbows on the table or speak with their mouths full.

7. When I called my little sister a brat, she stared at me with an expression of _____.

8. Even when their captain gave them a direct order to fire, the _____ soldiers did not raise their weapons.

Read to find out why Ralph wants to leave home.

Chapter 1 (cont.)

Questions:

1. How can you tell that Ralph's motorcycle is his most prized possession?

2. Why does Ralph keep his motorcycle under the grandfather clock?

3. Why does Ryan feel envious of Brad Kirby?

4. Why are Ryan and Matt able to understand Ralph when he speaks?

5. How can you tell that Matt cares about Ralph?

6. Why is Ralph anxious for the inn to close for the night?

7. What are some differences between Ralph's outdoor relatives and his indoor ones?

8. How do Ralph's relatives spoil his motorcycle rides?

9. Why does Ralph want to leave the Mountain View Inn?

Questions for Discussion:

1. Is Ralph "greedy," as his relatives say? Do you think he should share his motorcycle with his younger brothers, sisters, and cousins?

2. Have you ever been asked to share something that is precious to you?

3. Do you think Ralph should leave the Mountain View Inn?

Literary Devices:

I. *Personification*—Personification in literature is a device in which the author grants human qualities to nonhuman objects. For example:

> ...the clock began to grind and groan and strike, *bong... bong*, as if it had to summon strength for each stroke.

What is being personified?

_____

What mood does it create?

_____

_____

Chapter 1 (cont.)

II. *Onomatopoeia*—Onomatopoeia refers to the use of a word whose sound suggests its meaning. For example:

- wind <u>moaned</u>
- fire <u>crackled</u>
- <u>rattle</u> and <u>crunch</u> of a car with chains

What are some other examples of onomatopoeia?

_____

_____

_____

_____

Social Studies Connections:

1. Do some research to learn about the hieroglyphs, or pictographic script, of ancient Egypt. Find out how it differs from our own script. What languages today use pictographs in their script?
2. Do some research to learn how the Rosetta stone, found in 1799, led to the decipherment of ancient Egyptian hieroglyphs.

Writing Activity:

Imagine that you are Ralph. Write a letter of apology to your youngest indoor cousin's mother for having called her child a "rotten little rodent." Explain how you lost your temper.

CHAPTERS 2, 3

Vocabulary: Synonyms are words with similar meanings. Draw a line from each word in column A to its synonym in column B. Then use the words in column A to fill in the blanks in the sentences below.

	A		B
1.	strenuous	a.	anger
2.	volunteer	b.	hips
3.	miracle	c.	difficult
4.	enthusiastic	d.	marvel
5.	displeasure	e.	experienced
6.	sophisticated	f.	blameless
7.	haunches	g.	excited
8.	innocent	h.	offer

. . . .

1. The police accidentally arrested a(n) _____ person.

2. You should not _____ to play on the team unless you have time to go to practice.

3. The squirrel sat on its _____ while it nibbled an acorn.

4. Fifth graders are far more _____ than kindergartners.

5. The hike was so _____ that we all slept well that night.

6. Everyone is very _____ about a class trip to the circus.

7. If you are late again, you will face your teacher's _____.

8. Each living thing is a(n) _____ of nature.

> Read to find out what happens when Ralph goes to school.

Chapters 2, 3 (cont.)

Questions:

1. Why does the manager of the inn threaten to fire Matt the handyman?

2. If Ralph stays at the Mountain View Inn, how might his relatives be harmed?

3. How does Ralph feel about leaving home?

4. Why does Ralph think Miss K will have toothpaste in school?

5. How does the class find out that Ryan has brought a mouse to school?

6. How does Miss K react to Ralph?

7. Why doesn't Ralph want to run through a maze for the class? Why does Ryan want Ralph to do so?

8. Why doesn't Ryan leave Ralph's motorcycle with the mouse when the boy leaves school at the end of the day?

Questions for Discussion:

1. When Ralph left home, he made a personal sacrifice: he gave up his own wishes for the good of all the other mice. Have you or anyone you know ever made a personal sacrifice?

2. Do you think Ryan should have taken Ralph's motorcycle home with him?

3. Do you think Ralph will show that he is really smart when he runs the maze? What are the talents required to run a maze quickly?

Art/Science Connection:

Use the example in Chapter Three to design your own maze. There should be only one possible route from the start to the exit. Include plenty of "dead ends." Trace your maze twice or make two photocopies of it. Then have a friend use a pencil to "run" through one copy of your maze. Do not give him or her a chance to study the maze before running it. Use a watch or clock with a second hand to time your friend's run. Next, predict how much your friend's time will improve as he or she runs your maze a second and third time. Find out if your predictions were correct.

Chapters 2, 3 (cont.)

Social Studies Connections:

1. Do some research to learn about the Gold Rush that brought adventurers to California in 1849. Also, find out if there really is a town called La Cucaracha in California.

2. Does your school have a name? If so, do some research to find out how your school got its name. If your school does not have a name, take a class survey to find out whom or what your school should be named after.

Writing Activities:

1. In *Ralph S. Mouse* the reader gets a "mouse's eye view" of an elementary school classroom. Imagine that Ralph comes to visit your classroom. Write about the things he sees, hears, touches, tastes, and feels. If he observes something that he has never seen before, how does he explain it to himself? Tell how Ralph came to your school, where he hides, and what happens when your teacher spots him. Does your teacher react as enthusiastically as Miss K?

2. Ralph's motorcycle is his most prized possession. Do you own a toy, a piece of sports equipment, an article of clothing, or another possession that you love? Write a poem about your prized possession. Make sure readers can tell why you love it so much. Draw a picture to go with your poem.

CHAPTERS 4–6

Vocabulary: Antonyms are words that have opposite meanings. Draw a line from each word in column A to its antonym in column B. Then use the words in column A to fill in the blanks in the sentences below.

A	B
1. nimbly	a. wakeful
2. sneer	b. calm
3. sulky	c. smile
4. tactful	d. defeated
5. flustered	e. neat
6. tousled	f. cheerful
7. drowsy	g. clumsily
8. triumphant	h. rude

. . . .

1. The hot weather made me feel so _____ that I took a nap.

2. When Pablo hit a home run to win the game, his teammates' _____ shouts rang out across the field.

3. It is not _____ to criticize someone in front of others.

4. The cat jumped _____ onto the kitchen counter.

5. Please comb your _____ hair before we go to the party.

6. My little sister becomes _____ when she does not get her way.

7. "That movie is for babies!" Sophie said with a _____.

8. If you study all week, you won't feel _____ during Friday's math test.

> Read to find out whether Ralph can run a maze.

Questions:

1. How does Ralph find food to eat on his first night at Irwin J. Sneed Elementary?

2. Why does Miss K want Ryan and Brad to work together on the maze? How does their partnership work out?

Chapters 4–6 (cont.)

3. Why doesn't Ralph like the students' mouse pictures and written work about mice.

4. How does Miss K react to her students' mouse projects? Why do you think she reacts this way?

5. Do the reporter and photographer from the *Cucaracha Voice* seem interested in Room 5's mouse exhibit? How can you tell?

6. Why does Ralph decide to run the maze his own way?

7. Why is Ryan "disgusted" by the way Ralph runs the maze?

8. How does Ralph's motorcycle break?

Questions for Discussion:

1. Do you think it is possible to make friends by having a possession that others admire? Is this the way friendships should be formed?

2. Do you suffer from "disappearing" socks at your home? If so, on what do you blame this problem?

3. Should Miss K have been critical, rather than accepting, of some of her students' work about mice?

4. Do you think Ralph was justified in being angry at Ryan?

Literary Connection:

Find a copy of a poem made famous by Robert Burns, the Scottish poet, that begins, "wee, sleekit, cow'rin, tim'rous beastie...". Determine why Ralph would not have been pleased with the poem if he had understood its meaning.

Writing Activities:

1. A haiku is a Japanese-style poem that consists of three lines that do not rhyme. A traditional haiku has five syllables in the first line, seven in the second, and five in the last. (The number of words does not matter.) Write a haiku about Ralph or another mouse. Your haiku should capture a brief moment in the mouse's life. Before you write your poem, read some other haiku to help you appreciate this writing style.

2. Listen to a few songs on a country music radio station. Then write the lyrics to a sad country song that Ralph might have written.

CHAPTERS 7, 8

Vocabulary: Read each group of words. Cross out the one word that does not belong with the others. On the line below the words, tell how the rest of the words are alike.

1. invader   guest   intruder   burglar

   These words are alike because _____

   _____

2. outraged   furious   angry   content

   These words are alike because _____

   _____

3. expressing   voicing   concealing   saying

   These words are alike because _____

   _____

4. gifted   clever   bright   sympathetic

   These words are alike because _____

   _____

5. indignity   honor   embarrassment   humiliation

   These words are alike because _____

   _____

6. pondering   brooding   skulking   considering

   These words are alike because _____

   _____

7. thug   bully   brute   scuffle

   These words are alike because _____

   _____

   | Read to find out whether Ryan and Brad become friends. |

Chapters 7, 8 (cont.)

Questions:

1. Why is Ralph in a "forgiving mood" after the weekend?

2. Why does the class vote against having Ralph run the maze again?

3. Why does the *Cucaracha Voice* reporter write that Irwin J. Sneed Elementary School is "overrun" with mice?

4. What makes Ralph realize that a strand of Miss K's hair is useless?

5. Why does Ralph decide to speak to Brad? Why can Brad understand Ralph?

6. How did Ryan and Brad each come to think of the other as conceited or stuck-up?

Questions for Discussion:

1. Do you think Miss K should have discussed Ryan and Brad's fight in class?

2. Do you think Brad and Ryan will become friends? What story clues make you think so?

Language Study: Idioms

An idiom is an expression that does not mean exactly what it says. For example, if someone says, "I really have my hands full," it means that someone has a lot of work to do or has a tough problem to solve. What does Ralph mean when he tells himself that it is time to "take matters into his own paws"?

_____

_____

Science Connection:

Do some research to learn about animals, such as mice, that are nocturnal. Work with a partner to make lists of nocturnal animals and diurnal animals. Compare your lists with those of your classmates. Then discuss which of the nocturnal animals might be found in your locale.

Reader's Theater

Ralph and Brad's conversation in Chapter Eight is so dramatic that it might be performed as Reader's Theater. Work with two classmates. Assign the roles of Ralph and Brad; these performers will read all of the text within quotation marks. You will read the connecting narrative. Begin with "Ralph ran up Brad's leg...." and end with "...slipped under the door into the empty classroom." Rehearse the scene and present it to the rest of your class. Use your tone of voice and "body language" to express Ralph's fury and Brad's reluctance to reveal why he is so lonely.

Chapters 7, 8 (cont.)

Writing Activities:

1. Write about a time when you formed a mistaken first impression of someone, as Ryan and Brad did about each other. Tell what you first thought of the person and how you figured out that you were wrong. Also explain what led you to form inaccurate ideas about the person in the first place.

2. Brad reveals that he is lonely because he does not live with his mom anymore. Write a poem about a time when you missed someone or felt lonely or homesick.

3. Imagine you are Brad. Write a journal entry that describes how you felt when Ralph spoke to you.

CHAPTER 9, EPILOGUE

Vocabulary: Use the words in the Word Box and the clues below to fill in the crossword puzzle.

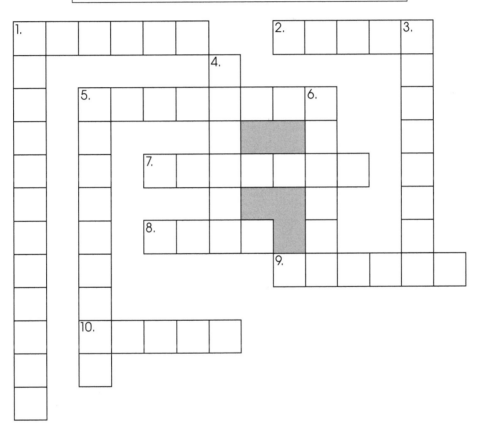

WORD BOX

altitude	maneuver	resent
conversation	miniature	rowdy
crouch	parka	rubbish
humble	peer	stayed

Across:
1. stoop; bend low
2. warm, hooded jacket
5. guide; steer
7. trash; garbage
8. look searchingly; peep
9. remained
10. disorderly; ill-behaved

Down:
1. exchange of thoughts by spoken words
3. the height of anything; extent or distance upward
4. unassuming; modest
5. reduced in size; tiny
6. feel or show displeasure or indignation

Read to find out whether this story has a happy ending.

Chapter 9, Epilogue (cont.)

Questions:

1. Why do the students in Miss K's class write letters to the editor of the *Cucaracha Voice*?

2. Why doesn't Ralph want to go back to the Mountain View Inn?

3. How do you know that Ryan and Brad have become friends?

4. Why do Ryan and Brad take Ralph back to the Mountain View Inn? How do they make his return a happy occasion?

5. How does Ralph put his new sports car into reverse?

6. Why isn't Ralph as pleased as Ryan and Brad by the retraction letter in the *Cucaracha Voice*?

7. How do the lessons he learned from Miss K help Ralph manage his rowdy young relatives?

Questions for Discussion:

1. Why do you think Ryan and Brad might think of Miss K as a teacher and a friend?

2. How do you think Ryan and Brad will get along as brothers?

3. At the end of a typical fairy tale, the heroes "live happily ever after." Does this story end happily? Do fairytale endings ever happen in real life?

Word Study: Word Parts

An *epilogue*—like the one at the end of *Ralph S. Mouse*—is a short section at the end of a story that tells what happens to the characters after the main part of the plot is over. Use the following list of words to help you guess what the word part –*logue* means. Then use a dictionary that gives word origins to find out whether you guessed correctly.

- dialogue
- prologue
- monologue
- logbook
- catalog
- travelogue

Chapter 9, Epilogue (cont.)

Literary Elements:

I. *Characterization*—In the chart below, compare Ryan at the beginning of the story to Ryan at the end of the story. Then make the same comparison for Ralph.

Character	Beginning of Story	End of Story
Ryan		
Ralph		

II. *Reality and Fantasy*—Most writers of fantasy ground their works in reality. This helps the reader accept the book's fantasy. Use the chart below to list story events and details that are realistic and events that could not happen in real life.

Realistic Story Elements	Fantastic Story Elements

Chapter 9, Epilogue (cont.)

Writing Activity:

Use a business letter form, such as the one below, to write the letter that Ryan might have written to the editor of the *Cucaracha Voice*. Alternatively, you may write a business letter to the editor of your local newspaper expressing a complaint of your own.

your name and address

_____
(date)

name, title, and address
of person/company
receiving the letter

Dear _____:

Body of letter

Sincerely yours,

_____
(name)

CLOZE ACTIVITY

The following passage is taken from Chapter Six. Read it through completely; then go back and fill in each blank with words that makes sense. When you are through, you may compare your words with those of the author.

After Mr. Costa left, the school was a silent, deserted place. The next morning the _____[1] did not return. Ralph, who did not _____[2] that there was no school on Saturday _____[3] Sunday, had never been so alone in _____[4] life. He stood in the cold and _____[5] hall and squeaked as loud as he _____,[6] but his tiny voice could not even _____[7] an echo. All weekend he roamed the _____[8] halls and classroom, half-heartedly nibbling whatever he _____[9] find to eat, going *pb-b-b* because he _____[10] his motorcycle so much, and wondering if _____[11] was doomed to roam forever the lonely _____[12] of the Irwin J. Sneed Elementary School. Why didn't the children _____?[13]

Ralph thought of the old hotel with _____[14] shabby lobby warmed by a crackling fire. _____[15] missed the reassuring tick of the rasping _____[16] clock. He missed watching television and the _____[17] in the lobby—the arrival and departure _____[18] guests and the arguments among the staff. _____[19] missed old Matt, his protector, and supplies _____[20] peanuts and popcorn from the Jumping Frog Lounge. He _____[21] if his plan to make the little _____[22] leave the lobby had worked and if _____[23] still had his job.

Ralph discovered he _____[24] missed—sort of—his little brothers and _____[25] and cousins. He wondered if the littlest _____[26] still fell over his own feet and _____[27] tangled in the fringe of the carpet. _____[28] wondered what they would say if they _____[29] see him now, cold and lonely, in _____[30] vast empty school. He also wondered what _____[31] would say if he went home with _____[32] without his motorcycle. Something like, "Yah, yah! Serves you right for not wanting to give us rides."

POST-READING QUESTIONS AND ACTIVITIES

1. Return to the story map in the Pre-Reading Activities on page three of this study guide. Complete the story map. Then compare your response with those of your classmates.

2. In a Venn diagram, such as the one below, compare the characters of Ryan and Brad. In the overlapping section, tell how the two boys are alike.

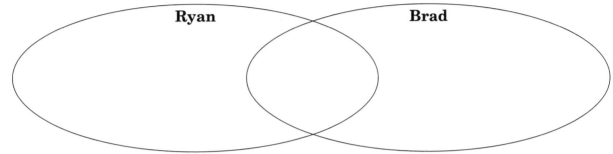

3. With a partner, gather information about BMX bicycles, motocross racing, and other kinds of races, such as the Tour de France bicycle race. Display your findings on a classroom bulletin board.

4. Write a letter to a friend in another class or school. Tell him or her about reading *Ralph S. Mouse.* Describe what you liked most about the book. Explain why you think your friend might like to read the book, too.

5. Pick your favorite scene from *Ralph S. Mouse.* Draw a comic strip that shows the scene. Your comic strip should have five or six panels. Write a sentence or two to go in each panel. If there is dialogue in your scene, write some of it in the characters' speech balloons.

6. Read one of the other books, written by Beverly Cleary, about Ralph S. Mouse. Compare that book with the one you have just read. Which book do you prefer? Do you think the books must be read in the order they were written, or does each book stand alone?

7. Find several picture books that feature mouse characters, such as *If You Give a Mouse a Cookie,* by Laura Joffe Numeroff or *Anatole,* by Eve Titus. Use a library computer catalog to help you search. Host a "Marvelous Mouse Day" on which you and your classmates read mouse books aloud to kindergartners and first graders at your school. Serve mouse-related snacks such as cheese and crackers to your young visitors.

8. Recall some other books you have read that take place in school. In a chart, such as the one below, tell what a main character in each story learns. Begin with *Ralph S. Mouse.*

Title	Character	What the Character Learns
Ralph S. Mouse	Ralph	

SUGGESTIONS FOR FURTHER READING

* Atwater, Richard, and Florence Atwater. *Mr. Popper's Penguins*. Little, Brown.
* Avi. *Poppy*. HarperCollins.
* Burnford, Sheila. *The Incredible Journey*. Random House.
* Butterworth, Oliver. *The Enormous Egg*. Little, Brown.
* Dahl, Roald. *James and the Giant Peach*. Penguin.
* Howe, James, and Deborah Howe. *Bunnicula*. Simon & Schuster.
* King-Smith, Dick. *A Mouse Called Wolf*. Random House.
* _____. *Babe, the Gallant Pig*. Random House.
  _____. *Martin's Mice*. Random House.
* Lewis, C.S. *The Lion, the Witch, and the Wardrobe*. HarperCollins.
* Naylor, Phyllis. *Shiloh*. Random House.
* Norton, Mary. *The Borrowers*. Harcourt.
* O'Brien, Robert C. *Mrs. Frisby and the Rats of NIMH*. Simon & Schuster.
* Peterson, John. *The Littles*. Scholastic.
* Selden, George. *The Cricket in Times Square*. Random House.
  Sharp, Margery. *Miss Bianca*. Little, Brown.
  _____. *The Rescuers*. Little, Brown.
* Taylor, Theodore. *The Trouble with Tuck*. Random House.
* White, E.B. *Charlotte's Web*. HarperCollins.
* _____. *Stuart Little*. HarperCollins.
* _____. *Trumpet of the Swan*. HarperCollins.
* Williams, Margery. *The Velveteen Rabbit*. HarperCollins.

Some Other Books by Beverly Cleary
* *Dear Mr. Henshaw*. HarperCollins.
  Ellen Tebbits. HarperCollins.
  Henry and Ribsy. HarperCollins.
* *Henry Huggins*. HarperCollins.
* *Muggie Maggie*. HarperCollins.
  Otis Spofford. HarperCollins.
* *Ramona Forever*. HarperCollins.
* *Ramona Quimby, Age 8*. HarperCollins.
* *Ramona the Brave*. HarperCollins.
  Ribsy. HarperCollins.
* *Socks*. HarperCollins.
* *Strider*. HarperCollins.

Additonal Books about Ralph
* *The Mouse and the Motorcycle*. HarperCollins.
  Runaway Ralph. HarperCollins.

* NOVEL-TIES Study Guides are available for these titles.

ANSWERS

Chapter 1

Vocabulary: 1. d 2. e 3. a 4. c 5. b 6. h 7. g 8. f; 1. rodents 2. winced 3. venture 4. retired 5. keen 6. civilized 7. reproach 8. defiant

Questions: 1. It is clear that Ralph's motorcycle is his most prized possession because he cannot wait to ride it each night. He keeps it in a safe place so his relatives won't take it, he cleans it carefully with Kleenex when it gets dirty, and he feels upset when he realizes it is wearing out. 2. Ralph keeps his motorcycle under the clock because this is the only place where it will be safe from his relatives who are scared of the clock's loud "bonging" noise. They think the clock is alive and is "out to get them." 3. Ryan is envious of Brad because he has a BMX bike and a dad who drives him to school in his tow truck. 4. Ryan and Matt can understand the mouse because they both conform to the criteria needed—being lonely and liking fast cars and motorcycles. Matt can understand Ralph completely because he cares about the mouse and "takes the trouble to listen." 5. It is clear that Matt cares about Ralph because he calls him "a mouse in a million," brings him popcorn, and helps Ralph by shooing his bothersome relatives away. 6. Ralph is anxious for the inn to close for the night so that he can ride his motorcycle in the lobby. 7. Ralph's outdoor relatives are bolder, rowdier, and meaner than his indoor ones, who are more timid and have better manners. 8. Ralph's relatives spoil his rides by getting in his way, asking for rides, and telling him he is greedy because he won't share his motorcycle. 9. Ralph wants to leave so he can get away from his relatives. He feels guilty about losing his temper with them and shocking the little indoor mice. Also he probably wants to be able to ride his motorcycle in peace.

Chapters 2, 3

Vocabulary: 1. c 2. h 3. d 4. g 5. a 6. e 7. b 8. f; 1. innocent 2. volunteer 3. haunches 4. sophisticated 5. strenuous 6. enthusiastic 7. displeasure 8. miracle

Questions: 1. The manager threatens to fire Matt because Ralph and his relatives have left muddy tracks and mouse droppings in the lobby. The manager blames Matt because he is responsible for keeping the lobby clean. 2. If Ralph stays at the inn and keeps riding his motorcycle, his relatives will continue creating a mess in the lobby. Then the manager might use mousetraps or cats to kill the mice. 3. Ralph feels sad about leaving Matt and frightened and bewildered about leaving home. He also feels brave and noble because he is protecting his relatives by leaving. 4. Ralph thinks Miss K has toothpaste at school because the only other teacher he has ever seen was in a toothpaste commercial on television. 5. The students notice Ralph when he pokes his head out of Ryan's pocket to get some air. 6. Miss K enthusiastically welcomes Ralph, calling him "a little miracle." She is so excited about the mouse's visit that she organizes a classroom mouse exhibit. 7. Ralph doesn't want to run through a maze for the class because he doesn't think a mouse who can ride a motorcycle should have to prove how smart he is. Also, he worries that he won't do well at this task. Ryan wants Ralph to run the maze because he wants to show off his mouse's brilliance. Ryan is a new kid at school, and no one paid much attention to him until he brought Ralph to class. 8. Ryan takes the motorcycle home so Ralph won't use it to ride all over the school and risk getting into trouble. Also, Ryan uses the motorcycle to bribe Ralph, saying he won't return it until the mouse agrees to run the maze.

Chapters 4–6

Vocabulary: 1. g 2. c 3. f 4. h 5. b 6. e 7. a 8. d; 1. drowsy 2. triumphant 3. tactful 4. nimbly 5. tousled 6. sulky 7. sneer 8. flustered

Questions: 1. On his first night at school, Ralph eats the beans and rice that are part of a student project, a jar of library paste, and a bag of sugar. 2. Miss K hopes Ryan and Brad will become friends if they work together. They each seem to need a friend. Their partnership does not work out well: they quarrel about how difficult the maze should be, and Brad calls Ralph "dumb." 3. Ralph thinks the mouse pictures are too big. He finds the written work silly, insulting, and frightening. One student writes that mice are harmful, and another writes a scary haiku poem about a mouse dying in a trap. 4. Miss K says something positive about each student's work. She probably does this to be encouraging to her students. Also, she is an enthusiastic teacher who does not seem to believe in negativity of any kind. 5. The reporter and photographer come late and leave early. This makes it seem as if they are not very interested in the mouse exhibit. 6. Ralph is angry and embarrassed because he keeps banging into the partitions as he tries to run the maze in the conventional way. Also, other food odors make it difficult for him to smell the peanut butter at the end of the maze so he cheats by jumping to the top of the maze. 7. Ryan is disgusted because he wants Ralph to run the maze the usual way. If Ralph had succeeded, Ryan thinks, it would have made his classmates look up to him and like him. 8. Ralph's motorcycle breaks because it is in Ryan's pocket when Ryan and Brad get into a fight. Ryan falls down and the motorcycle snaps in half.

Chapters 7, 8

Vocabulary: 1. guest—the other words all name people who enter without permission 2. content—the other words all describe angry feelings 3. concealing—the other words are all synonyms for communicating 4. sympathetic—the other words are all synonyms for smart 5. honor—the other words all relate to feelings of shame 6. skulking—the other words are all synonyms for thinking 7. scuffle—the other words all name people who like to fight.

Questions: 1. Ralph is so glad to see the class after his lonely weekend that it puts him in a "forgiving mood." 2. The class decides that Ralph should not have to run the maze again because the unusual way he ran the maze the first time shows that he is "gifted and talented." 3. After paying only a short visit to Room 5, the reporter exaggerates and twists the information in order to make the story more exciting. 4. When Ralph finally sees how badly damaged his motorcycle is, he realizes that even a strand of Miss K's strong hair will not repair it. 5. Ralph decides to speak to Brad because he is very angry with the boy for breaking his motorcycle. Brad can understand the mouse because he is Ralph's "type," a lonely boy who likes fast cars and motorcycles. 6. Ryan thinks of Brad as conceited because he envies Brad for having a BMX bike, a dog, and a dad who drives a tow truck. Brad's unfriendliness may make him seem conceited, too. Brad mistakenly assumes that because Ryan lives in a hotel, he must be rich.

Chapter 9, Epilogue

Vocabulary: Across—1. crouch 2. parka 5. maneuver 7. rubbish 8. peer 9. stayed 10. rowdy; Down—1. conversation 3. altitude 4. humble 5. miniature 6. resent

Questions: 1. The students in Miss K's class write letters to the editor of the *Cucaracha Voice* to express their displeasure over the article about the mouse exhibit. They believed the information was based on conjecture rather than fact. 2. Ralph doesn't want to go back to the Mountain View Inn because he fears that his relatives will make fun of him for returning without his motorcycle. 3. It is clear that Ryan and Brad have laid aside their differences and are now friends when they collaborate on a surprise for Ralph. They also make plans to visit each other at home. 4. Ryan and Brad bring Ralph back to the Mountain View Inn because he cannot spend the rest of his life in the school; staying there might present a danger to his life and cause him to be lonely on weekends and vacations. The boys make Ralph happy upon his return by giving him the Laser XL7 toy sports car that Brad has outgrown as a toy, but the mouse finds even better than the motorcycle that was broken. 5. To back up the car, Ralph says *moorv*, which is the reverse of *vroom*, the noise he makes to move forward. 6. Although the boys are happy to see Ryan's name in the newspaper in the article about their class, Ralph is upset because he was referred to as Ryan's pet, not as the independent spirit he thought himself to be. 7. From Miss K, Ralph learned patience. When his relatives demand rides in his new car, Ralph has them form a line so they can take turns. He has also learned to say positive, supportive things to them to encourage good behavior.